SRA Open Court Reading

Level 1 • Book 2

Being Afraid

•

Homes

SRA OpenCourt READING

Level 1 • Book 2

— PROGRAM AUTHORS —

Marilyn Jager Adams Jan Hirshberg Marsha Roit
Carl Bereiter Anne McKeough Marlene Scardamalia
Joe Campione Michael Pressley Gerald H. Treadway, Jr.

A Division of The McGraw·Hill Companies

Columbus, Ohio

Acknowledgments

Grateful acknowledgment is given to the following publishers and copyright owners for permissions granted to reprint selections from their publications. All possible care has been taken to trace ownership and secure permission for each selection included. In case of any errors or omissions, the Publisher will be pleased to make suitable acknowledgments in future editions.

Being Afraid
My Brother Is Afraid of Just About Everything by Lois Osborn. Copyright © 1982. Reprinted by permission of Multimedia Product Development, Inc., Chicago, Illinois.
From WE'RE GOING ON A BEAR HUNT. Text copyright © 1989 by Michael Rosen, illustrations copyright © 1989 by Helen Oxenbury. First published in 1989 by Walker books Ltd. London. Reprinted with permission of Margaret K. McElderry Books, Simon & Schuster Children's Publishing Division. All rights reserved. Canadian rights: WE'RE GOING ON A BEAR HUNT. Text © Copyright 1989 Michael Rosen; Illustrations © 1989 Helen Oxenbury. Reproduced by permission of Candlewick Press Inc., Cambridge, MA.
"Strange Bumps" from OWL AT HOME by Arnold Lobel. COPYRIGHT © 1975 BY ARNOLD LOBEL. Used by permission of HarperCollins Publishers.
From CLYDE MONSTER by Robert L. Crowe, illustrated by Kay Chorao. Text copyright © 1976 by Robert L. Crowe, 1976. Illustrations Copyright © Kay Sproat Chorao, 1976. Used by permission of Dutton Children's Books, a division of Penguin Putnam Inc.
"The Cat and the Mice" from THE BEST OF AESOP'S FABLES Text © Copyright 1990 by Margaret Clark; Illustrations © 1990 by Charlotte Voake. Reproduced by permission of Candlewick Press Inc., Cambridge, MA on behalf of Walker Books Ltd., London.

IRA SLEEPS OVER by Bernard Waber. Copyright © 1972 by Bernard Waber. Reprinted by permission of Houghton Mifflin Co. All rights reserved.
"Something Is There" from SPOOKY RHYMES AND RIDDLES by Lilian Moore. Copyright © 1972 Lilian Moore. Used by permission of Marian Reiner for the author.

Homes
BUILDING A HOUSE COPYRIGHT © 1981 BY BYRON BARTON. Used by permission of HarperCollins Publishers.
From A HOUSE IS A HOUSE FOR ME written by Mary Ann Hoberman, illustrated by Betty Fraser. Text copyright © Mary Ann Hoberman, 1978. Illustrations copyright © Betty Fraser, 1978. Published by arrangement with Viking Children's Books, a division of Penguin Putnam, Inc.
From ANIMAL HOMES, text copyright © 1991 by Illa Podendorf. Reprinted by permission of Children's Press, a division of Grolier Publishing.
"Make a Home" from Nancy Pemberton's ANIMAL HABITATS: The Best Home of All, "Make A Home" copyright 1990 by The Child's World, Chanhassen, MN. Reprinted with permission of copyright holder.
HOME FOR A BUNNY written by Margaret Wise Brown, illustrated by Garth Williams © 1956, renewed 1984 Golden Books Publishing Company, Inc. All rights reserved. Reprinted by permission.
From IS THIS A HOUSE FOR HERMIT CRAB? by Megan McDonald, illustrated by S.D. Schindler. Published by Orchard Books, an imprint of Scholastic Inc. Text copyright © 1990 by Megan McDonald, illustrations copyright © 1990 by S.D. Schindler. Reprinted by permission.
THE THREE LITTLE PIGS by Margot Zemach. Copyright © 1989 by Margot Zemach. Reprinted by permission of Farrar, Straus & Giroux, LLC.

Photo Credits

8 (tl) Nicholas DeVore/Tony Stone Images, (br) © Leonard Lee Rue/Photo Researchers, Inc.; 34 © Lois Osborn; 68 Philadelphia Museum of Art. Gift of Mrs. John D. Rockefeller; 69 (t) The Metropolitan Museum of Art, Catharine Lorillard Wolfe Collection, Wolfe Fund, 1906 (06.1234) Photograph © 1995 The Metropolitan Museum of Art, (b) Amon Carter Museum, Fort Worth, Texas. 1961.231; 82 (t) © Merle Fox Photography, (b) © Kay Chorao; 88 (b) © Walker Books Limited; 138 (tl) © Robert Frerck/The Stock Market, 138 (tr) © Nicholas DeVore/Tony Stone Images, (b) © Blair Seitz/Photo Researchers, Inc.; (t) © Wolfgang Kaehler/Corbis, (b) © Focus/Moller/Woodfin Camp & Associates; 140 (t) © Robert Frerck/Woodfin Camp & Associates, (b) © Dan Budnik/Woodfin Camp & Associates, (br) © Adam Woolfitt/Woodfin Camp & Associates; 141 (t) © Traveler's Resource/Tony Stone Images, (b) © Momatiuk/ Eastcott/Woodfin Camp & Associates; 142 (t) © Harry Gruyaert/Magnum Photos, Inc.,(b) © Porterfield/Chickering/Photo Researchers, Inc.; 143 (t) © Craig Aurness/Woodfin Camp & Associates, (b) © David Hiser/Tony Stone Images; 144 (t) © Hilarie Kavanagh/Tony Stone Images, (b) © David Stoecklein/The Stock Market; 145 (t) © Paul Chesley/National Geographic Society Image Collection, (b) © John F. Mason/The Stock Market; 146 (t) © Charles & Josette Lenars/Corbis, (b) © Mike Yamashita/Woodfin Camp & Associates; 147 (t) © Martin Rogers/Tony Stone Images, (b) © E. Spiegelhalt/Woodfin Camp & Associates; 148 (t) © Nicholas DeVore/Tony Stone Images, (b) © E G Company; 149 © Hilarie Kavanagh/Tony Stone Images; 180 © Oxford Scientific Films/Animals Animals; 181 © Dwight R. Kuhn/DRK Photo; 182 © Leonard Lee Rue/Photo Researchers, Inc.; 183 © PHOTRI, (b) © Oxford Scientific Films/Animals Animals; 184 © W. Perry Conway/Tom Stack & Associates; 185 © John Gerlach/Tom Stack & Associates; 186 © Alan G. Nelson/Dembinsky Photo Associates; 187 © W. Perry Conway/Tom Stack & Associates; 188 © Ernest Wilkinson/Animals Animals; 189 © Doug Wechsler/Animals Animals; 191 © Jeff Foott/DRK Photo; 192 (t) © Dominique Braud/Tom Stack & Associates, (b) © Wendy Shattil/Bob Rozinski/Tom Stack & Associates; 193 © E.R. Degginger/Photo Researchers, Inc.; 194 (tl) © E.R. Degginger/Animals Animals, (tr) © John Gerlach/Animals Animals, (bl) © Carl R. Sams II/Dembinsky Photo Associates, (br) © Stan Osolinski/Dembinsky Photo Associates; 195 (tl) © Stephen J. Krasemann/Photo Researchers, Inc., (tr) © David T. Roberts/Nature Images, Inc./Photo Researchers, Inc., (bl) © E.R. Degginger/Animals Animals, (br) © Richard Kolar/Animals Animals; 196 © W. Perry Conway/Tom Stack & Associates; 198 (t) Collection of the Artist. Photo: Suzanne Kaufman, (b) National Gallery of Canada, Ottawa, Ontario, Canada; 199 (t) Edwin and Virgin Irwin Memorial Collection, Cincinnati Art Museum, (c) Canadian Museum of Civilization, (b) © Giraudon/Art Resource, NY; 204 © Barbara Bruno; 218 (t) © Morgan Collection/Archive Photos.

Unit Opener Illustrations

10–11 Lisa McCue; 136–137 Loretta Krupinski.

www.sra4kids.com

SRA/McGraw-Hill
A Division of The McGraw-Hill Companies

Send all inquiries to:
SRA/McGraw-Hill
8787 Orion Place
Columbus, Ohio 43240-4027

Printed in the United States of America.

ISBN 0-07-569243-0

6 7 8 9 RRW 05 04 03

Program Authors

Marilyn Jager Adams, Ph.D.
BBN Technologies

Carl Bereiter, Ph.D.
University of Toronto

Joe Campione, Ph.D.
University of California at Berkeley

Jan Hirshberg, Ed.D.
Reading Specialist

Anne McKeough, Ph.D.
University of Calgary

Michael Pressley, Ph.D.
University of Notre Dame

Marsha Roit, Ph.D.
National Reading Consultant

Marlene Scardamalia, Ph.D.
University of Toronto

Gerald H. Treadway, Jr., Ed.D.
San Diego State University

Table of Contents

UNIT 10

Table of Contents

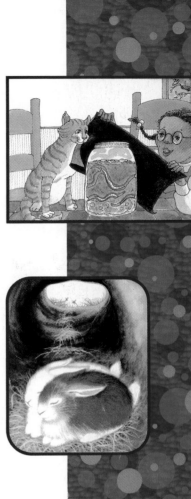

Being Afraid

Being afraid is not fun, but everyone is afraid sometimes. What do you do when you are afraid? What do your friends do? The story characters you will meet in this unit find many different things to be afraid of. See what they do when they are afraid.

My Brother Is Afraid of Just About Everything

Lois Osborn
illustrated by Loretta Krupinski

My little brother is afraid of just about everything. Whenever there's a thunderstorm, I know where to find him.

Underneath the bed.

When we're outside and the mailman
comes, I know where to find him.
Behind the bushes.
He doesn't like men with beards.

When he's in the bathtub, he
screams if I let the water out. Maybe
he thinks he'll go down the drain along
with the water.

So I take him out first. Then I empty
the tub.

Yesterday my mother started to vacuum. My brother started to howl.
    Maybe he thinks the vacuum cleaner is a monster. He sure acts that way. So my mother asked me to take him for a walk.

We went past my school. "See?" I said. "That's where you'll be going in a couple of years."

I could tell by my brother's face what he thought about *that*.

We met some of my friends at the playground. They think my brother is cute. "What's your name?" and "How old are you?" they asked.

Did my brother answer them?
No-o-o, of course not.
He just buried his face in my
stomach, the way he always does.

On our way home, we came to some railroad tracks. A train was coming, so we waited to cross.

Most kids think trains are pretty exciting. They wave at the engineer. They count cars. But not my brother.

His arms went around me like
boa constrictors. I couldn't have
shaken him loose if I'd wanted to.

Back home, we sat together under the big tree in our backyard. I decided it was time we had a talk.

"Look," I said to him, "did thunder and lightning ever hurt you?" He shook his head.

"Or the mailman, or the vacuum cleaner?" He shook his head again.

"Then how come you're so scared of everything?" I asked.

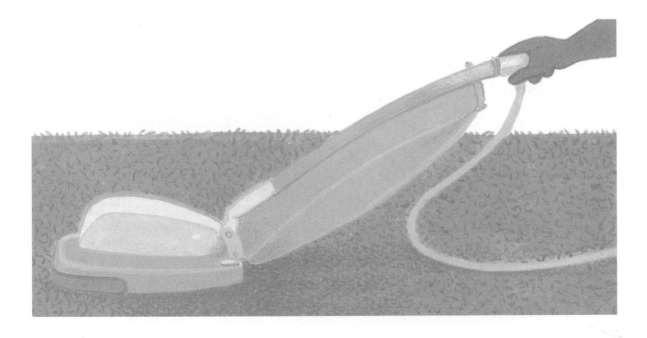

My brother's face drooped. The corners of his mouth turned down and quivered. His shoulders came up to his ears. His big eyes looked at me.

I felt like patting him on the back and saying that everything was okay.

But instead I said, "Look, you've got to get tough. It's stupid to keep on being afraid of things that won't hurt you."

Then I saw a great big, happy smile spread across my brother's face. He was looking at something behind me. I didn't even have to ask what it was.

Nothing else could make my brother
look that happy. It had to be—a dog!

I tried. I tried very hard.

I shut my eyes and pretended the dog wasn't there.

I took deep breaths so my heart wouldn't beat so fast.

I clenched my hands so they would stop trembling.

I prayed the dog would go away.

28

Then I felt its feet upon my shoulders. I thought of sharp claws.

I felt its rough, wet tongue against the back of my neck. I thought of all those teeth.

That did it!

I couldn't get into the house fast enough! Across the yard I ran. I yanked open the screen door and quickly slammed it shut. I even hooked it.

Safe behind the door, I stood, catching my breath.

Then I went to the window. I knew
what I would see.
   Yes, there was my brother, with his
arms around that dog.

I watched them play together. I watched them for a long time.

I suppose that dog would have played with me, too, if I had been outside.

But I stayed inside.
I felt bad about it, but I stayed inside.
Oh well, everybody's afraid of
something, I guess.

My Brother Is Afraid of Just About Everything

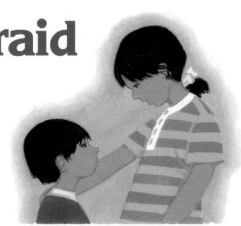

Meet the Author

Lois Osborn was a teacher for 26 years. She started writing after she retired. She likes to visit schools to read her books and talk about writing.

Meet the Illustrator

Loretta Krupinski began drawing as a very young child and has never stopped. She has created marine paintings of boats and lighthouses for many years. Recently, she began illustrating and writing children's picture books. Krupinski enjoys going back and forth between real-life marine paintings and children's picture books.

Theme Connections

Within the Selection

Read the questions below, and think about your answers. In small groups, discuss your ideas with one another. Then choose a person to report your group's answers to the class.

- What made the boy afraid of so many things?
- What was funny about the way the sister tried to help?

Beyond the Selection

- Think about fears you have had and how you got over them.
- Add items to the Concept/Question Board about being afraid.

Focus Questions Do you like spiders? Why or why not? What would you do if you saw a spider next to you?

Little Miss Muffet

Nursery Rhyme
illustrated by Dominic Catalano

Little Miss Muffet sat on her tuffet,
Eating her curds and whey;
Along came a spider and sat down beside her
And frightened Miss Muffet away.

We're Going on a Bear Hunt

Retold by Michael Rosen
illustrated by Helen Oxenbury

We're going on a bear hunt.
We're going to catch a big one.
What a beautiful day!
We're not scared.

Oh-oh! Grass!
Long, wavy grass.
We can't go over it.
We can't go under it.

Oh, no!
We've got to go through it!

Swishy swashy!
Swishy swashy!
Swishy swashy!

We're going on a bear hunt.
We're going to catch a big one.
What a beautiful day!
We're not scared.

Oh-oh! A river!
A deep, cold river.
We can't go over it.
We can't go under it.

40

We're going on a bear hunt.
We're going to catch a big one.
What a beautiful day!
We're not scared.

Oh-oh! Mud!
Thick, oozy mud.
We can't go over it.
We can't go under it.

42

Oh, no!
We've got to go through it!

Squelch squerch!
Squelch squerch!
Squelch squerch!

43

We're going on a bear hunt.
We're going to catch a big one.
What a beautiful day!
We're not scared.

Oh-oh! A forest!
A big, dark forest.
We can't go over it.
We can't go under it.

Oh, no!
We've got to go through it!

Stumble trip!
Stumble trip!
Stumble trip!

We're going on a bear hunt.
We're going to catch a big one.
What a beautiful day!
We're not scared.

Oh-oh! A snowstorm!
A swirling, whirling snowstorm.
We can't go over it.
We can't go under it.

Oh, no!
We've got to go through it!

Hoooo woooo!
Hoooo woooo!
Hoooo woooo!

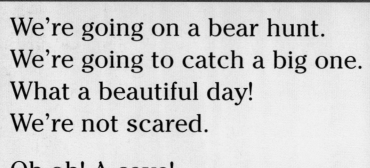

We're going on a bear hunt.
We're going to catch a big one.
What a beautiful day!
We're not scared.

Oh-oh! A cave!
A narrow, gloomy cave.
We can't go over it.
We can't go under it.

Oh, no!
We've got to go through it!

Tiptoe!
Tiptoe!
Tiptoe!
WHAT'S THAT?

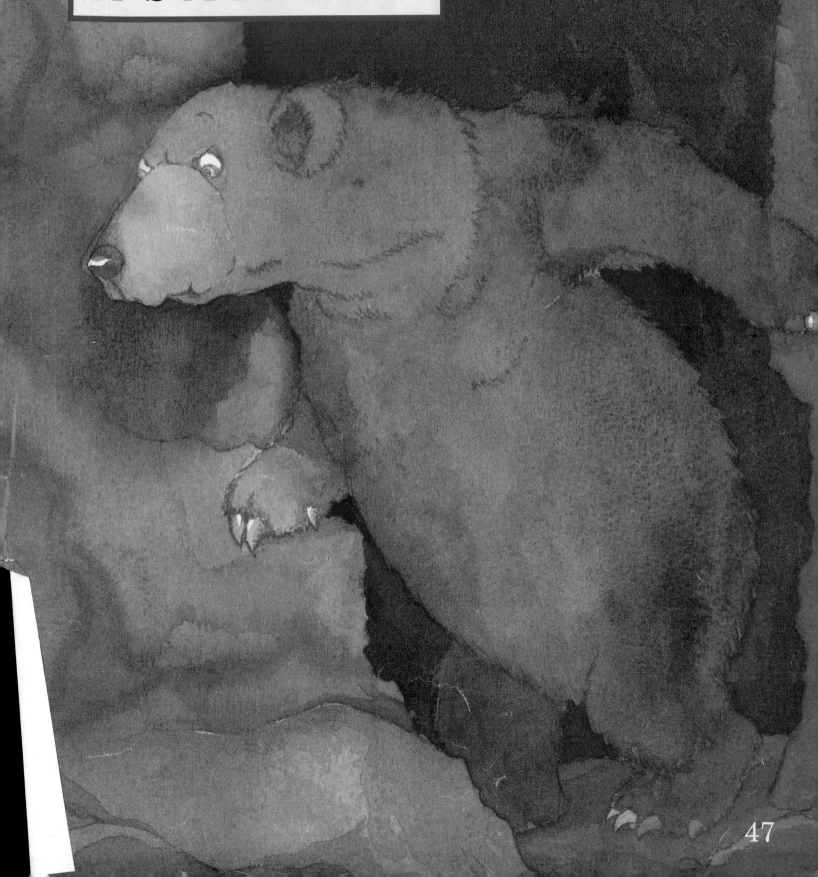

One shiny wet nose!
Two big furry ears!
Two big goggly eyes!

IT'S A BEAR!!!!

Quick! Back through the cave! Tiptoe! Tiptoe! Tiptoe!

Back through the snowstorm! Hoooo wooooo! Hoooo wooooo!

Back through the forest! Stumble trip! Stumble trip! Stumble trip!

Back through the mud! Squelch squerch! Squelch squerch!

Back through the river! Splash splosh! Splash splosh! Splash splosh!

Back through the grass! Swishy swashy! Swishy swashy!

Get to our front door.
Open the door.
Up the stairs.

Oh, no!
We forgot to shut the door.
Back downstairs.

Shut the door.
Back upstairs.
Into the bedroom.

Into bed.
Under the covers.

We're not going on

a bear hunt again.

We're Going on a Bear Hunt

Meet the Author

Michael Rosen has many talents. He is a poet, performer, broadcaster, and scriptwriter. He has been writing children's books since 1970.

Meet the Illustrator

Helen Oxenbury has won many awards for her illustrations. She lives in London, England, with her husband, John Burningham, who is also an award-winning illustrator.

Theme Connections

Within the Selection

Read the questions below and think about your answers. In small groups, discuss your ideas with one another. Then choose a person to report your group's answers to the class.

- How did the family feel before they saw the bear?
- How do you know the family was afraid of the bear when they saw it?

Across Selections

- What did both the family and Little Miss Muffet do when they were afraid?

Beyond the Selection

- What animals are scary to you?
- Add items to the Concept/Question Board about being afraid.

Focus Questions Why are people afraid of
the dark sometimes? Have you ever thought
you've seen something in the dark,
and it was not really there?

Strange Bumps

Arnold Lobel

Owl was in bed. "It is
time to blow out the
candle and go to sleep,"
he said with a yawn.

Then Owl saw two
bumps under the blanket
at the bottom of his bed.
"What can those strange
bumps be?" asked Owl.

54

Owl lifted up the blanket. He looked down into the bed. All he could see was darkness. Owl tried to sleep, but he could not.

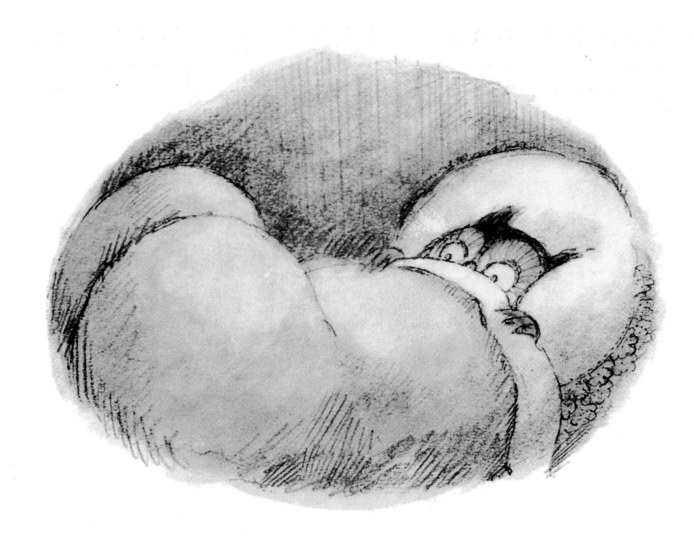

"What if those two strange bumps grow bigger and bigger while I am asleep?" said Owl. "That would not be pleasant."

Owl moved his right foot up and
down. The bump on the right moved
up and down. "One of those bumps is
moving!" said Owl.

Owl moved his left foot up and
down. The bump on the left moved up
and down. "The other bump is
moving!" cried Owl.

Owl pulled all of the covers off his bed. The bumps were gone. All Owl could see at the bottom of the bed were his own two feet.

"But now I am cold," said Owl. "I will cover myself with the blankets again."

As soon as he did, he saw the same two bumps.

"Those bumps are back!" shouted
Owl. "Bumps, bumps, bumps! I will
never sleep tonight!"

Owl jumped up and down on top of his bed.

"Where are you? What are you?" he cried. With a crash and a bang the bed came falling down.

Owl ran down the stairs. He sat in
his chair near the fire.

"I will let those two strange bumps sit on my bed all by themselves," said Owl. "Let them grow as big as they wish. I will sleep right here where I am safe."

And that is what he did.

Strange Bumps

Meet the Author and Illustrator

Arnold Lobel was born in Los Angeles, California. When he was a child, he often told stories and drew pictures to go with these stories to amuse his classmates. He would also put on his own plays at home. Arnold Lobel studied at an art college, then he began his career in children's books. He wrote and illustrated more than 100 books.

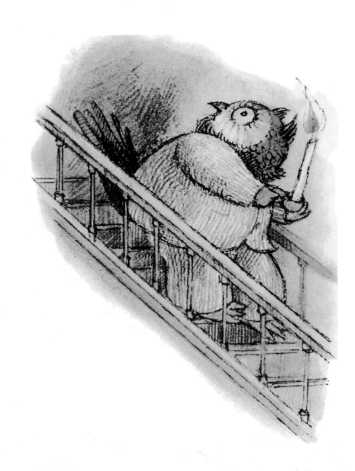

Theme Connections

Within the Selection

Read the questions below, and think about your answers. In small groups, discuss your ideas with one another. Then choose a person to report your group's answers to the class.

- What was Owl afraid of?
- How did Owl get over his fear?

Across Selections

- How was Owl braver than the other characters you read about?

Beyond the Selection

- Think about bedtime fears you may have had. How did you get over them?
- Add items to the Concept/Question Board about being afraid.

Cat trying to catch a goldfish. c. 1838–1840. **Utagawa Kuniyoshi.** Color woodcut. Philadelphia Museum of Art.

The Gulf Stream. 1899. **Winslow Homer.** Oil on canvas.
$28 \frac{1}{8} \times 49 \frac{1}{8}$ in. The Metropolitan Museum of Art, New York, NY.

His First Lesson. 1903. **Frederic Remington.** Oil on canvas.
Amon Carter Museum, Fort Worth, Texas.

Focus Questions What fears have you tried to get over?
How did you do it?

Clyde Monster

Robert L. Crowe

illustrated by Kay Chorao

C lyde wasn't very old, but he was
growing—uglier every day. He lived
in a large forest with his parents.

Father Monster was a big, big monster and very ugly, which was good. Friends and family usually make fun of a pretty monster. Mother Monster was even uglier and greatly admired. All in all, they were a picture family—as monsters go.

Clyde lived in a cave. That is, he was
supposed to live in a cave, at night anyway.
During the day, he played in the forest,
doing typical monster things like breathing
fire at the lake to make the steam rise.

He also did typical Clyde things like turning somersaults that made large holes in the ground, and generally bumping into things. He was more clumsy than the average monster.

At night, Clyde was supposed to go to his cave and sleep. That's when the trouble started. He refused to go to his cave.

"Why?" asked his mother. "Why won't you go to your cave?"

"Because," answered Clyde, "I'm afraid of the dark."

"Afraid," snorted his father until his nose burned. "A monster of mine afraid? What are you afraid of?"

"People," said Clyde. "I'm afraid there are people in there who will get me."

"That's silly," said his father. "Come, I'll show you." He breathed a huge burst of fire that lit up the cave. "There. Did you see any people?"

"No," answered Clyde. "But they may be hiding under a rock and they'll jump out and get me after I'm asleep."

"That is silly," pointed out his mother with her pointed tongue. "There are no people here. Besides, if there were, they wouldn't hurt you."

"They wouldn't?" asked Clyde.

"No," said his mother. "Would you ever hide in the dark under a bed or in a closet to scare a human boy or girl?"

"Of course not!" exclaimed Clyde, upset that his mother would even think of such a thing.

"Well, people won't hide and scare you either. A long time ago monsters and people made a deal," explained his father. "Monsters don't scare people, and people don't scare monsters."

"Are you sure?" Clyde asked.

"Absolutely," said his mother. "Do you know of a monster who was ever frightened by a people?"

"No," answered Clyde after some thought.

"Do you know of any boys or girls who were ever frightened by a monster?"

"No," he answered quickly.

"There!" said his mother. "Now off to bed."

"And no more nonsense about being scared by people," ordered his father.

"Okay," said Clyde as he stumbled into
the cave. "But could you leave the rock
open just a little?"

Clyde Monster

Meet the Author

Robert L. Crowe used to be a teacher. Then he became a superintendent of schools. He wrote "Clyde Monster" to help his own children overcome their fear of the dark.

Meet the Illustrator

Kay Chorao is from Indiana. Now she lives in New York City. As a child, Kay loved to draw. As soon as she was old enough to hold a crayon, she "scribbled drawings over every surface," including the breakfast room table!

Theme Connections

Within the Selection

Read the questions below, and think about your answers. In small groups, discuss your ideas with one another. Then choose a person to report your group's answers to the class.

- What was Clyde Monster afraid of?
- How did Clyde's parents help him?

Across Selections

- In which other story does an older person try to help a younger person with a fear?

Beyond the Selection

- Think of a time when another person helped you get over a fear. What happened?
- Add items to the Concept/Question Board about being afraid.

Focus Questions Why would a mouse want to stay away from a cat? Do animals get scared sometimes?

The Cat and the Mice

Aesop
retold by Margaret Clark
illustrated by Charlotte Voake

A family of mice was being chased every day by a hungry cat.

"What are we going to do?" said Mother, as they all sat around her one evening.

Everyone had something to suggest, but the smallest mouse said, "If we hang a bell around his neck, then we shall hear him coming and we'll have time to get out of his way."

All the mice squealed in excitement and told the smallest mouse how clever he was.

Then the oldest mouse in the family spoke. "That may *sound* like a good idea," he said, "but tell me: which one of you is brave enough to go up to the cat and hang a bell around his neck?"

87

The Cat and the Mice

Meet the Author

Margaret Clark started to write when her children were young. As they grew, she changed the age levels of her stories. She says, "I write for young people and of course for myself. Most of my books grow out of my own experiences." Margaret likes to write about things she has done, like camping.

Meet the Illustrator

Charlotte Voake always wanted to be an illustrator. She won a poster contest when she was twelve. Voake published her first book while she was still in college. She lives in England and enjoys sailing when she isn't drawing.

Theme Connections

Within the Selection

Read the questions below, and think about your answers. In small groups, discuss your ideas with one another. Then choose a person to report your group's answers to the class.

- What did the smallest mouse want to do?
- Why did the oldest mouse not like the plan?

Across Selections

- How was the mouse's plan different from what the characters in other stories did about their fears?

Beyond the Selection

- Think of a time you made something seem less scary. What happened?
- Add items to the Concept/Question Board about being afraid.

Ira Sleeps Over

by Bernard Waber

I was invited to sleep at Reggie's house. Was I happy! I had never slept at a friend's house before.

But I had a problem. It began when
my sister said: "Are you taking your
teddy bear along?"

"Taking my teddy bear along!" I said.
"To my friend's house? Are you kidding?
That's the silliest thing I ever heard!
Of course, I'm not taking my teddy bear."

And then she said: "But you never slept without your teddy bear before. How will you feel sleeping without your teddy bear for the very first time? Hmmmmmmm?"

"I'll feel fine. I'll feel great. I will
probably love sleeping without my teddy
bear. Just don't worry about it," I said.
"Who's worried?" she said.

93

But now, she had me thinking about it. Now, she really had me thinking about it. I began to wonder: Suppose I won't like sleeping without my teddy bear. Suppose I just hate sleeping without my teddy bear. Should I take him?

"Take him," said my mother.
"Take him," said my father.
"But Reggie will laugh," I said.
"He'll say I'm a baby."
"He won't laugh," said my mother.
"He won't laugh," said my father.
"He'll laugh," said my sister.
I decided not to take my teddy bear.

That afternoon, I played with Reggie. Reggie had plans, big plans. "Tonight," he said, "when you come to my house, we are going to have fun, fun, fun.

96

First, I'll show you my junk collection.
And after that we'll have a wrestling
match. And after that, a pillow fight.
And after that we'll do magic tricks.
And after that we'll play checkers.
And after that we'll play dominoes.
And after that we can fool around
with my magnifying glass."

"Great!" I said. "I can hardly wait."
"By the way," I asked, "what do you
think of teddy bears?"

But Reggie just went on talking and planning as if he had never heard of teddy bears. "And after that," he said, "do you know what we can do after that—I mean when the lights are out and the house is really dark? Guess what we can do?"

"What?" I asked.

"We can tell ghost stories."

"Ghost stories?" I said.

"Ghost stories," said Reggie, "scary, creepy, spooky ghost stories."

I began to think about my teddy bear.

"Does your house get
very dark?" I asked.
"Uh-huh," said Reggie.
"Very, very dark?"
"Uh-huh," said Reggie.
"By the way," I said again, "what do
you think of teddy bears?"

Suddenly, Reggie was in a big hurry
to go someplace. "See you tonight,"
he said.

"See you," I said.

I decided to take my teddy bear.
"Good," said my mother.
"Good," said my father.

But my sister said: "What if Reggie wants to know your teddy bear's name. Did you think about that? And did you think about how he will laugh and say Tah Tah is a silly, baby name, even for a teddy bear?"

"He won't ask," I said.

"He'll ask," she said.

Reggie sighed.

I sighed.

"We can still tell ghost stories,"
said Reggie.

"Do you know any?" I asked.

"Uh-huh," said Reggie.

Reggie began to tell a ghost story: "Once there was this ghost and he lived in a haunted house only he did most of the haunting himself. This house was empty except for this ghost because nobody wanted to go near this house, they were so afraid of this ghost. And every night this ghost would walk around this house and make all kinds of clunky, creeky sounds. *Aroomp! Aroomp!* Like that. And he would go around looking for people to scare because that's what he liked most to do: scare people. And he was very scary to look at. Oh, was he scary to look at!"

Reggie stopped. "Are you scared?"
he asked.

"Uh-huh," I said. "Are you?"

"What?" said Reggie.

"Are you scared?"

"Just a minute," said Reggie, "I have to
get something."

"What do you have to get?" I asked.

"Oh, something," said Reggie.

Reggie pulled the something out of a
drawer. The room was dark, but I could
see it had fuzzy arms and legs and was
about the size of a teddy bear. I looked
again. It was a teddy bear.

Reggie got back into bed. "Now,
about this ghost . . ." he said.
   "Is that your teddy bear?" I asked.
   "What?" said Reggie.
   "Is that your teddy bear?"
   "You mean this teddy bear?"
   "The one you're holding," I said.
   "Uh-huh," Reggie answered.
   "Do you sleep with him all of
the time?"
   "What?" said Reggie.
   "Do you sleep with him all of
the time?"
   "Uh-huh."

"Does your teddy bear have a name?
Does your teddy bear have a name?" I
said louder.

"Uh-huh," Reggie answered.

"What is it?"

"You won't laugh?" said Reggie.

"No, I won't laugh," I said.

"Promise?"

"I promise."

"It's Foo Foo."

"Did you say 'Foo Foo'?"

"Uh-huh," said Reggie.

"Just a minute," I said, "I have to get something."

"What do you have to get?" Reggie asked.

"Oh, something," I answered.

The next minute, I was ringing my own doorbell. The door opened.

"Ira!" everyone said. "What are you doing here?"

"I changed my mind," I answered.

"You what!" said my mother.

"You what!" said my father.

"You what!" said my sister. (She was still up.)

"I changed my mind," I said. "I decided to take Tah Tah after all."

114

I went upstairs. Soon, I was down
again with Tah Tah.

My sister said: "Reggie will laugh.
You'll see how he'll laugh. He's just
going to fall down laughing."

"He won't laugh," said my mother.

"He won't laugh," said my father.

"He won't laugh," I said.

I came back to Reggie's room. "I have a teddy bear, too," I said. "Do you want to know his name?" I waited for Reggie to say, Uh-huh. But Reggie didn't say, Uh-huh. Reggie didn't say anything. I looked at Reggie. He was fast asleep. Just like that, he had fallen asleep.

"Reggie! Wake up!" I said. "You have to finish telling the ghost story." But Reggie just held his teddy bear closer and went right on sleeping. And after that–well, there wasn't anything to do after that. "Good night," I whispered to Tah Tah. And I fell asleep, too.

Ira Sleeps Over

Meet the Author and Illustrator

Bernard Waber loves to write about family problems. He uses funny characters to tell about things that might happen to you or me. He is best known for his books about a crocodile named Lyle. Waber's funny illustrations make children and grown-ups laugh out loud!

Theme Connections

Within the Selection

Read the questions below, and think about your answers. In small groups, discuss your ideas with one another. Then choose a person to report your group's answers to the class.

- Why did Ira not take his teddy bear at first?
- What made Ira decide to get his teddy bear?

Across Selections

- In what other story did a character feel afraid at bedtime?

Beyond the Selection

- Think about times you stay in a new place.
- Add items to the Concept/Question Board about being afraid.

Focus Questions How do you feel when you are afraid? Have you ever heard something that made you afraid?

Something Is There

Lilian Moore
illustrated by Toni Goffe

Something is there
there on the stair
coming down
coming down
stepping with care.
Coming down
coming down
slinkety-sly.
Something is coming and
wants to get by.

Focus Questions Do you know any folktales
about being afraid? Has a person younger than you
been afraid of something and you've helped them?

The Three Billy Goats Gruff

a folktale retold by
Christine Crocker

illustrated by
Holly Hannon

Once upon a time there were
three billy goat brothers named Gruff.
The three billy goats lived by a river.
Across the river was a meadow with
tall green grass.

One day, the billy goats wanted to
cross the river to eat the grass. But
there was only one bridge across the
river. And under that bridge lived a
mean, hungry troll. The troll had

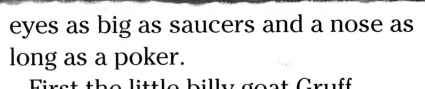

eyes as big as saucers and a nose as long as a poker.

First the little billy goat Gruff started across the bridge. His little feet went trip trap, trip trap on the bridge. The troll heard the noise.

"Who's that trip-trapping over my bridge?" roared the troll.

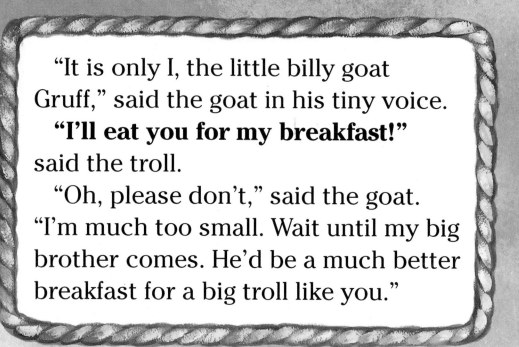

"It is only I, the little billy goat Gruff," said the goat in his tiny voice. **"I'll eat you for my breakfast!"** said the troll.

"Oh, please don't," said the goat. "I'm much too small. Wait until my big brother comes. He'd be a much better breakfast for a big troll like you."

"Very well," said the greedy troll. So he let the little billy goat Gruff cross the bridge.

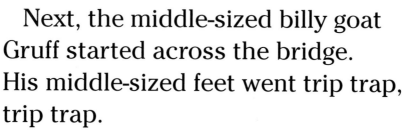

Next, the middle-sized billy goat Gruff started across the bridge. His middle-sized feet went trip trap, trip trap.

"Who's that trip-trapping over my bridge?" shouted the troll.

"It's only I, the middle-sized billy goat Gruff," said the goat in his middle-sized voice.

"I'll eat you for my breakfast!" roared the troll. And he jumped up on the bridge.

"Oh, please don't," said the goat. "I'm much too small. Wait for my big brother. He'd be a much better meal for a big troll like you."

"Very well," said the greedy troll.
So he let the middle-sized billy goat
Gruff cross the bridge.

Soon the big billy goat Gruff started across the bridge. His big feet went trip trap, trip trap. The bridge shook.

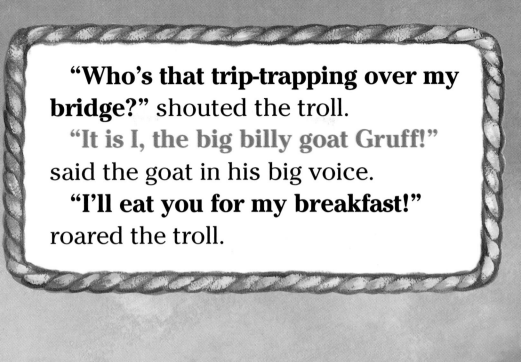

"**Who's that trip-trapping over my bridge?**" shouted the troll.

"It is I, the big billy goat Gruff!" said the goat in his big voice.

"**I'll eat you for my breakfast!**" roared the troll.

"Oh no, you won't," said the goat.
The big billy goat Gruff ran at the troll
and butted him into the river. The
troll was never heard of again.

Then the three billy goats Gruff went into the meadow. They ate all the grass they wanted and lived happily ever after. And so—
Snip, snap, snout,
This tale's told out.

The Three Billy Goats Gruff

Meet the Illustrator

Holly Hannon has worked as a professional illustrator for many years. Her works come from the joy found in brilliant colors and beautiful surroundings. She lives with her husband in Seneca, South Carolina, where she enjoys gardening, hiking, cooking, and reading about all three.

Theme Connections

Within the Selection

Read the questions below, and think about your answers. In small groups, discuss your ideas with one another. Then choose a person to report your group's answers to the class.

- What were the three billy goats afraid of?
- What did the billy goats do about their fear?

Across Selections

- In what story did characters plan to trick a character they were afraid of?

Beyond the Selection

- Think of a time when you outsmarted something or someone you were afraid of. What happened?
- Add items to the Concept/Question Board about being afraid.

Are all homes alike? Would a good home for a bunny be a good home for a bird or a crab? What makes a good home for all the different people and animals in the world?

Homes Around the World

by Deborah Eaton

Argentina

Lesotho, South Africa

The Philippines

Here you will see many homes
and many faces in many different
far-off places.

138

Cliff houses are cool
when the sun is hot.

Mali

It's not too
hot here.
Grass grows
on a roof.

Germany

139

A reed hut is made of dried plants.

Peru

You need a ladder to get to some pueblo houses.

New Mexico, USA

Flowers make this home pretty.

Austria

Their house is up on stilts.

The Philippines

His house has a tin roof.

Poland

141

Trailers are homes on wheels.

Nevada, USA

Some homes float.

Hong Kong

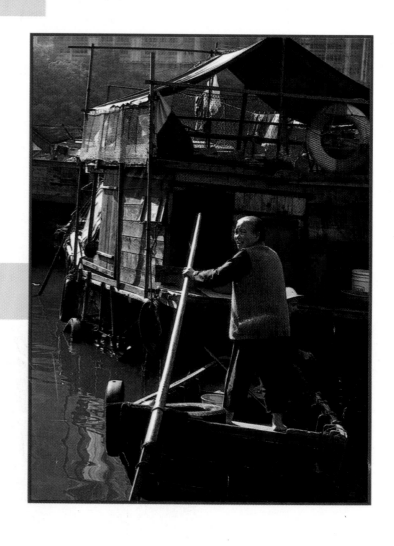

Some homes fold right up.

Morocco

People can even turn palm leaves into a home.

Guatemala

A porch is a nice place to sit.

Thailand

A fireplace warms a home.

New Mexico, USA

144

Doors are for friends coming in.

China

Windows let light in and let people smile out.

Argentina

145

Big and tall . . .

Indonesia

Round and small . . .

Somalia

146

All over the world, homes are for living . . .

Sudan

and homes are for enjoying.

Utah, USA

Homes Around the World

Meet the Author and Photographer

Deborah Eaton decided to become a writer when she was sixteen years old. She has written *No One Told the Aardvark the Elephants Are Coming*, *Where Is My Baby?*, and *The Family Tree*. Deborah Eaton lives in Maine and has a cat named Pudge who sits in the window and waves at people as they pass by the house. She loves to write about animals and is working on a new book.

148

Theme Connections

Within the Selection

Read the questions below, and think about your answers. In small groups, discuss your ideas with one another. Then choose a person to report your group's answers to the class.

- How are the homes in the pictures different?
- How are the homes the same?

Beyond the Selection

- Think about your home. What do you like about it?
- Add items to the Concept/Question Board about homes.

Building a House

by Byron Barton

On a green hill a bulldozer digs
a big hole.

The workers leave.

The house is built.

The family moves inside.

Building a House

Meet the Author and Illustrator

Byron Barton became known as "the artist" in grade school. He got the name because he often painted pictures. He said, "My pictures were hanging all over the back walls of the class." He grew up to write and illustrate stories about how to do things like build a house, put together dinosaur bones, and travel on a spaceship.

Theme Connections

Within the Selection

Read the questions below, and think about your answers. In small groups, discuss your ideas with one another. Then choose a person to report your group's answers to the class.

- Why does it take so many people to build a house?
- Why must you build a house in a special sequence?

Across Selections

- Would the steps in "Building a House" be used for all the houses in "Homes Around the World"? Why?

Beyond the Selection

- Think about your house. What other steps might be needed to build it?
- Add items to the Concept/Question Board about homes.

A House is a House for Me

Mary Ann Hoberman
illustrated by Betty Fraser

A hill is a house for an ant, an ant.
A hive is a house for a bee.
A hole is a house for a mole or a mouse
And a house is a house for me!

158

A web is a house for a spider.

A bird builds its nest in a tree.

There is nothing so snug as a bug
in a rug

And a house is a house for me!

159

A coop? That's a house for a chicken.
A sty? That's a house for a sow.
A fold? That's where sheep all gather
to sleep.
A barn? That's a house for a cow.
(It is also, of course,
A house for a horse.)

My dog has fleas

A kennel's a house for a dog, a dog.
A dog is a house for a flea.
But when a dog strays, a flea
sometimes stays
And then it may move in on me!

161

Houses for rabbits are hutches.
A house for a mule is a shed.
A castle's a house for a duchess.
A bedbug beds down in a bed.

Mosquitoes like mudholes or puddles.
Whales need an ocean or sea.
A fish or a snake may make do with
a lake
But a house is a house for me!

A shell is a dwelling for shellfish:
For oysters and lobsters and clams.
Each snail has a shell and each
turtle as well
But not any lions or lambs.
Lions live out in the open.
Monkeys live up in a tree.
Hippos live down in a river.
Now what do you know about me?

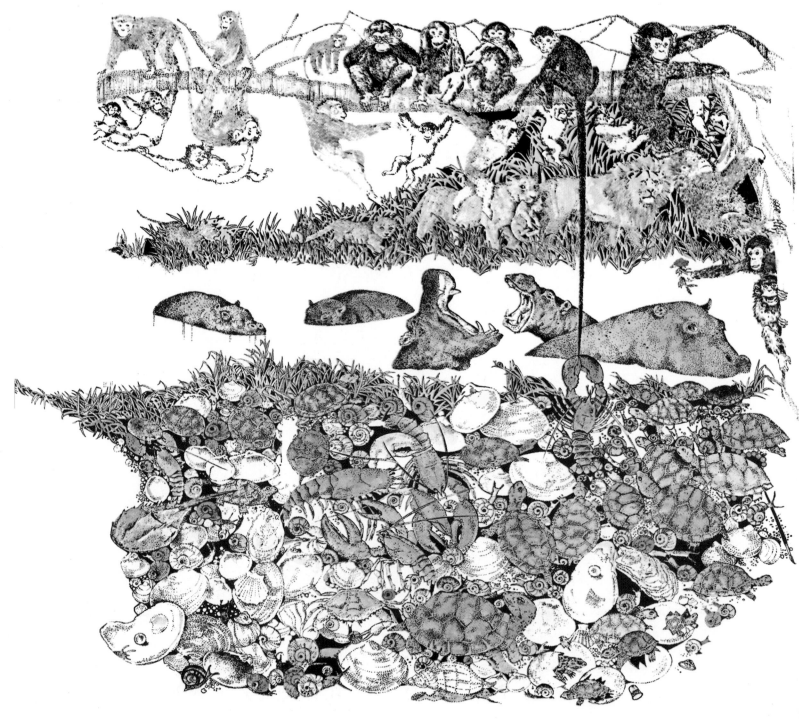

An igloo's a house for an Eskimo.
A tepee's a house for a Cree.
A pueblo's a house for a Hopi.
And a wigwam may hold a Mohee.

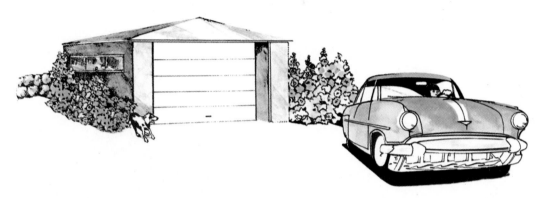

A garage is a house for a car or a truck.

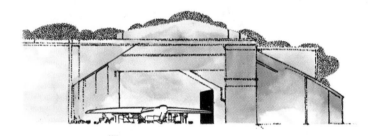

A hangar's a house for a plane.

A dock or a slip is a house for a ship

And a terminal's house for a train.

A husk is a house for a corn ear.
A pod is a place for a pea.
A nutshell's a hut for a hickory nut
But what is a shelter for me?

A glove is a house for a hand, a hand.
A stocking's a house for a knee.
A shoe or a boot is a house for a foot
And a house is a house for me!

A box is a house for a teabag.
A teapot's a house for some tea.
If you pour me a cup and I drink it all up,
Then the teahouse will turn into me!

Cartons are houses for crackers.
Castles are houses for kings.
The more that I think about houses,
The more things are houses for
things.
And if *you* get started in thinking,
I think you will find it is true
That the more that you think
about houses for things,

The more things are houses to *you*.

Barrels are houses for pickles
And bottles are houses for jam.
A pot is a spot for potatoes.
A sandwich is home for some ham.

The cooky jar's home to the cookies.
The breadbox is home to the bread.
My coat is a house for my body.
My hat is a house for my head.

Perhaps I have started farfetching . . . .
Perhaps I am stretching things some . . . .
A mirror's a house for reflections . . . .
A throat is a house for a hum . . . .
But once you get started in thinking,
You think and you think and you think
How pockets are houses for pennies
And pens can be houses for ink;

penny pincher

How peaches are houses for peachpits
And sometimes are houses for worms;
How trashcans are houses for garbage
And garbage makes houses for germs;

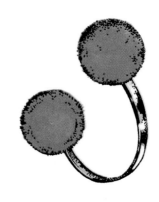

And envelopes, earmuffs and eggshells
And bathrobes and baskets and bins
And ragbags and rubbers and roasters
And tablecloths, toasters and tins . . .

And once you get started in thinking
this way,
It seems that whatever you see
Is either a house or it lives in a house,
And a house is a house for me!

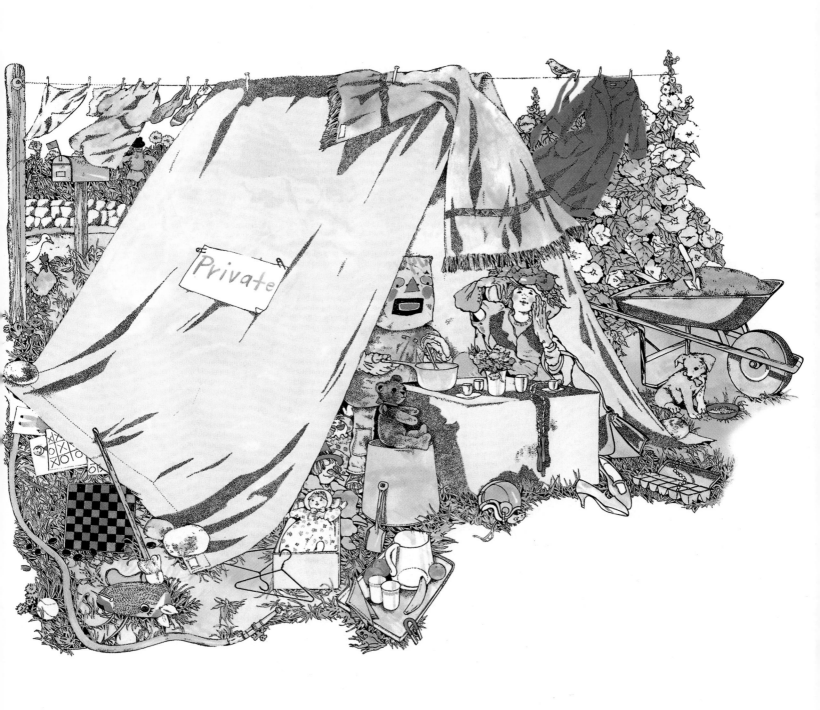

A book is a house for a story.
A rose is a house for a smell.
My head is a house for a secret,
A secret I never will tell.

A flower's at home in a garden.
A donkey's at home in a stall.
Each creature that's known has a
house of its own
And the earth is a house for us all.

A House Is a House For Me

Meet the Author

Mary Ann Hoberman liked thinking up stories, poems, and songs when she was a little girl. She would make up words for her poems to the rhythm of her swing. When she became a mother, she made up stories for her four children. Now she writes for you and me!

Meet the Illustrator

Betty Fraser won a coloring contest when she was seven years old. She got a two-dollar prize for coloring the best Easter egg! Now Betty Fraser likes to draw with a pen and ink. She likes to draw posters, cards, and book jackets. She thinks illustrating a long book would be very hard.

Theme Connections

Within the Selection

Read the questions below, and think about your answers. In small groups, discuss your ideas with one another. Then choose a person to report your group's answers to the class.

- Which houses in this story are the most interesting to you?
- What does a "house" mean in this story?

Across Selections

- What other stories talk about different kinds of homes?

Beyond the Selection

- Think about how this story makes you look differently at things.
- Add items to the Concept/Question Board about homes.

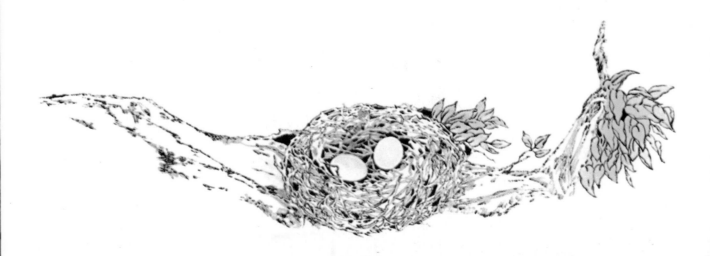

Animal Homes

Illa Podendorf

Many animals make their homes on top of the ground.

Cottontail rabbits make nests in fields in the spring.

Baby rabbits in nest

A cottontail's nest is warm. It is made from soft grass and lined with fur. The mother lines the nest with fur from her own body.

In winter, cottontails do not live in nests. Then they live under a barn or under some corn stalks.

Mice

Sometimes white-footed mice make their nests among plants on top of the ground.

A fox does not do much building to make its home. It finds a hollow log or a hole among the rocks and makes its den there.

Fox cubs in their den

Squirrel nest

Some animal homes are above the ground.

Sometimes squirrels make nests of twigs and leaves and grass in branches of trees.

Other times squirrels make homes in holes in trees. These homes are usually their winter homes.

Squirrel

Raccoons live near water in woods. Some raccoons make their homes in hollow trees.

Raccoon nest

A garden spider lives among plants. A garden spider spins a web. It stays on or near its web.

Spiderweb

Some animal homes are under the ground.

Ground squirrels build homes under the ground.

Their home is a long hall. This hall is called a tunnel. Sometimes the ground squirrels leave a pile of dirt at the door to their home.

Ground squirrel

Badgers live underground, too. If you look for them, it is easy to see where they dig their tunnels.

Badger den

Skunks often make their homes in holes in the ground. They sometimes dig new holes. But they may use a hole that some other animal has made. Sometimes skunks crawl under buildings and make their homes there.

Skunk nest

Some kinds of ants build their homes underground. They dig on and on until they have a long tunnel underground.

Ants digging a tunnel

Ants make more than one tunnel. At the end of each tunnel they make a room. In an ant home there are many tunnels and many rooms.

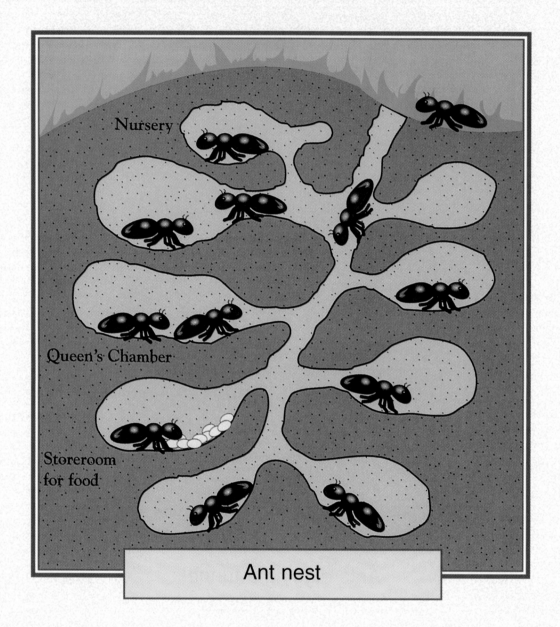

Nursery

Queen's Chamber

Storeroom for food

Ant nest

The first room to be made is a nursery. The baby ants live here.

Many of the rooms are storerooms for food. The worker ants bring back food to put in the storerooms.

Ants carrying food to the storeroom

Beaver lodge

Some animal homes are in water. Beavers build their homes in water. A beaver's home has a big room above water. The door to the home is underwater. A beaver swims underwater and up into the room of his home.

Beaver

Sunfish make a nest at the bottom of a pond. The father brushes a place clean with his fins. Then the mother fish lays her eggs. They both protect the nest from their enemies.

Sunfish

Woodchuck burrow

Chickadee nest

Remember, animals live in many places.
Some animals live in the ground.
Some animals live high above the ground.
Some animals live in water.
Other animals live on land.

Alligator and turtles

Elk

Deer

Horned toad

Some animals live in the woods.
Others live on the desert.
Some kinds of animals build
unusual homes.
Each animal home is just right for
the animal that builds and lives in it.

Spittlebug home

Hornet nest

195

Animal Homes

Meet the Author

Illa Podendorf was a science teacher and wrote science books for children. She believed that students should be creative and should be able to solve problems.

Theme Connections

Within the Selection

Read the questions below, and think about your answers. In small groups, discuss your ideas with one another. Then choose a person to report your group's answers to the class.

- Where are some places animals live?
- Why don't all animals live in the same kind of home?

Across Selections

- How are animal homes like homes for people?

Beyond the Selection

- Think of animals that are not in the story. What are their homes like?
- Add items to the Concept/Question Board about homes.

Part Two of My Village, in Yorubaland, Nigeria, Africa. c. 1980–1990. **Chief Z. K. Oloruntoba.** Plant dyes on fabric. Collection of the artist.

Shacks. 1919. **Lawren Harris.** Oil on canvas, 107.9 × 128 cm. National Gallery of Canada, Ottawa, Ontario, Canada.

Street Scene-Gloucester. c. 1940.
Edward Hopper. Oil on canvas.
Cincinnati Art Museum.

Making Tent for Winter. 1974.
Malaya Akulukjuk. Stencil print
by Solomon Karpik, Pangnirtung
Print Shop, 1975. Canadian
Museum of Civilization.

**Miniature funerary model of a
house.** Han dynasty, 202 BC–AD 220.
Chinese. Pottery. Musée Cernuschi,
Paris.

Focus Questions How can you make a
home for an animal? What would an animal
need in or near its home?

Make a Home

Nancy Pemberton
illustrated by Barbara Bruno

You can make a home for worms.
You will need:
- a big glass jar with a wide mouth
- loose soil
- pebbles mixed with soil
- earthworms
- lettuce and cornmeal for the worms
  to eat
- black paper and tape

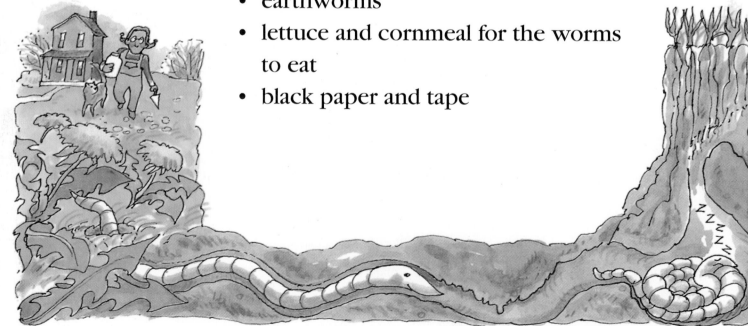

1. Fill the bottom of the jar with pebbles mixed with soil. Add loose soil to fill most of the jar. Keep the soil moist.

2. Put small pieces of lettuce and some cornmeal on top of the soil.

3. Dig up some earthworms and put them in the jar.

4. Tape black paper to the sides of the jar for one week. That will make the worms tunnel near the glass.

5. Take off the black paper.
    Watch how the worms
    move and eat.

6. When you are done
    watching the worms,
    return them to their
    outdoor home.

Make a Home

Meet the Illustrator

Barbara Bruno is a writer, artist, and photographer. She has illustrated stories in many books and magazines.

Theme Connections

Within the Selection

Read the questions below, and think about your answers. In small groups, discuss your ideas with one another. Then choose a person to report your group's answers to the class.

- What is a worm's home like?
- What will the worms think the black paper is?

Across Selections

- How is the worm's home like other homes you have read about?

Beyond the Selection

- Think about the worm's home. How might a worm help the soil that it lives in?
- Add items to the Concept/Question Board about homes.

Focus Questions What time of year are many animals born? Could a bunny live in a bird's home?

Home for a Bunny

Margaret Wise Brown

illustrated by Garth Williams

"Spring, Spring, Spring!" sang the frog.

"Spring!" said the groundhog.

"Spring, Spring, Spring!" sang the robin.

It was Spring.

The leaves burst out.

The flowers burst out.

And robins burst out of their eggs.

It was Spring.

In the Spring a bunny came down the road.
He was going to find a home of his own.
A home for a bunny,
A home of his own,
Under a rock,
Under a stone,
Under a log,
Or under the ground.
Where would a bunny find a home?

"Where is your home?"
he asked the robin.

"Here, here, here," sang the robin.
"Here in this nest is my home."

"Here, here, here," sang the little robins
who were about to fall out of the nest.
"Here is our home."

"Not for me," said the bunny.
"I would fall out of a nest.
I would fall on the ground."
So he went on looking for a home.

"Where is your home?" he asked the frog.

"Wog, wog, wog," sang the frog.

"Wog, wog, wog,
Under the water,
Down in the bog."

"Not for me," said the bunny.
"Under the water, I would drown in a bog."
So he went on looking for a home.

"Where do you live?" he asked the
groundhog.

"In a log," said the groundhog.

"Can I come in?" said the bunny.

"No, you can't come in my log,"
said the groundhog.

So the bunny went down the road.

Down the road and down the road he went.

He was going to find a home of his own.

A home for a bunny,

A home of his own,

Under a rock

Or a log

Or a stone.

Where would a bunny find a home?
Down the road
and down the road
and down the road
he went, until—

He met a bunny.
"Where is your home?"
he asked the bunny.
"Here," said the bunny.

"Here is my home.
Under this rock,
Under this stone,
Down under the ground,
Here is my home."

"Can I come in?" said the bunny.

"Yes," said the bunny.

And so he did.

And that was his home.

Home for a Bunny

Meet the Author

Margaret Wise Brown was born in New York City. She wrote about 100 books for children, as well as songs. She did not have many friends when she was a child, and she spent lots of time "in the woods and along the beaches and in the imaginary countries of the worlds I made up."

Meet the Illustrator

Garth Williams was born in New York City. Both of his parents were artists. He remembers that when he was growing up, "Everybody in my house was always either painting or drawing, so I thought there was nothing else to do in life but make pictures."

218

Theme Connections

Within the Selection

Read the questions below, and think about your answers. In small groups, discuss your ideas with one another. Then choose a person to report your group's answers to the class.

- What kind of home did the bunny need?
- Why was it hard for the bunny to find a home?

Across Selections

- What other story tells about a rabbit's home?

Beyond the Selection

- Think about an animal's body covering. What clues does it give to the kind of home the animal needs?
- Add items to the Concept/Question Board about homes.

Focus Questions Why would a hermit crab need to move to a different house? Where would be a good place for a hermit crab to live?

Is This a House for Hermit Crab?

Megan McDonald
illustrated by S. D. Schindler

Hermit Crab was forever growing too big for the house on his back. It was time to find a new house. He crawled up out of the water looking for something to hide in, where he would be safe from the pricklepine fish.

220

He stepped along the shore, by the sea, in the sand . . . *scritch-scratch, scritch-scratch* . . . until he came to a rock.

Is this a house for Hermit Crab?

Turning himself around, Hermit Crab
backed his hind legs beneath the rock.
The rock would not budge. It was
too heavy.

So he stepped along the shore, by the sea, in the sand . . . *scritch-scratch, scritch-scratch* . . . until he came to a rusty old tin can.

Is this a house for Hermit Crab?

When he tried to walk with the can on his back, it bumped and clunked. It was too noisy.

So he stepped along the shore, by the sea, in the sand . . . *scritch-scratch, scritch-scratch* . . . until he came to a piece of driftwood.

Is this a house for Hermit Crab?

Hermit Crab crawled deep inside the rounded hollow at one end. It was too dark.

So he stepped along the shore, by the sea, in the sand . . . *scritch-scratch, scritch-scratch* . . . until he came to a small plastic pail.

Is this a house for Hermit Crab?

Climbing up toward the rim, *oops!* he fell right in. He clawed, and he clawed, until he climbed back out. It was too deep.

So he stepped along the shore, by the sea, in the sand . . . *scritch-scratch, scritch-scratch* . . . until he came to a nice round hole in the sand.

Is this a house for Hermit Crab?
He poked his head down into the
opening. A huge pair of eyes blinked
back at him. Hermit Crab shivered as
he scurried away from the big fiddler
crab peering out of its burrow. It was
too crowded.

So he stepped along the shore, by the sea, in the sand . . . *scritch-scratch, scritch-scratch* . . . until he came to a fishing net.

Is this a house for Hermit Crab?

Poking his claws into the heap, he got tangled and caught. Hermit Crab wriggled and wriggled until he found his way out of the net. It had too many holes.

So he stepped along the shore, by the sea, in the sand . . . *scritch-scratch, scritch-scratch.* . . . All of a sudden a gigantic wave tossed and tumbled pebbles and sand over Hermit Crab's head. He swirled and whirled with the tide and was washed back out to sea.

Sleeker than a shark, the pricklepine fish darted out from its hiding place in the tall seaweed. Every spine on its back stood straight as a steeple. Mouth open wide, it headed right for Hermit Crab. Hermit Crab raced across the ocean floor . . . *scritch-scritch-scritch-scritch* . . . scurrying behind the first creature he saw.

It was a sea snail, and he hoped it would hide him, but the shell was empty. The shell was empty!

Hermit Crab scrambled inside as quick as a flash, and clamped his claw over the opening in the shell.

The pricklepine fish circled the snail shell three times, but he could not catch sight of the crab he had been chasing. He glided off in search of something else to eat.

When all seemed still and quiet, Hermit Crab snuggled comfortably

down into his new shell. It was not too heavy, not too noisy, not too dark, and not too deep. It was not too crowded and did not have too many holes.

At last, Hermit Crab had found a new home. And it fit just right.

Is This a House for Hermit Crab?

Meet the Author

Megan McDonald remembers growing up in "a house stuffed with books." She was the youngest of five girls, and they all liked to read books and tell stories, so there were always interesting dinnertime storytelling sessions. "As a writer, I try to tell stories that will invite children to reestablish a connection with themselves and their own imagination."

Meet the Illustrator

S. D. Schindler studied to become a doctor, but decided he wanted to be an artist instead. He enjoyed drawing when he was very young, and especially liked drawing animals. He was known as the class artist in school.

Theme Connections

Within the Selection

Read the questions below, and think about your answers. In small groups, discuss your ideas with one another. Then choose a person to report your group's answers to the class.

- Why did Hermit Crab quickly need a new house?
- Why did he take so long to find a new house?

Across Selections

- In which other story did an animal look for the right home?

Beyond the Selection

- How is the hermit crab's search for a house like a person's search for a house?
- Add items to the Concept/Question Board about homes.

Focus Questions What materials would you use to build a house? Why would it be important for someone to make a plan before building a house?

The Three Little Pigs

retold and illustrated by Margot Zemach

Long ago, three little pigs lived happily with their momma pig. But the day came when their momma told them it was time for them to go out into the world.

"Build good, strong houses,"
she said, "and always watch out
for the wolf. Now goodbye,
my sons, goodbye."

As the first little pig was going along, he met a man who was gathering straw.

"Please, sir," he said, "give me some straw to build me a house."

So the man gave him some straw
and the first little pig built himself
a house.

One day the wolf came knocking
at his door.

"Little pig, little pig," he called.
"Let me come in!"

But the first little pig said:
"No, no, I won't let you in—
not by the hair of my chinny-chin-chin."

"Well then," said the wolf,
"I'll huff and I'll puff and I'll blow
your house down."
   So he huffed and he puffed
and he blew the house down,
and he ate up the first little pig.
Yumm-yum!

As the second little pig was going
along, he met a man with a load
of sticks.

"Please, sir," he said, "give me
some sticks to build me a house."
So the man gave him some sticks
and the second little pig built
himself a house.

One day the wolf came knocking
at his door.

"Little pig, little pig," he called.
"Let me come in!"

But the second little pig said:
"No, no, I won't let you in—
not by the hair of my chinny-chin-chin."

"Well then," said the wolf,
"I'll huff and I'll puff
and I'll blow your house down."
So he huffed and he puffed
and he huffed and he puffed
and he blew the house down,
and he ate up the second little pig.
Yumm-yum!

As the third little pig was going along, he met a man with a load of bricks.

"Please, sir," he said, "give me some bricks to build me a house."

So the man gave him some bricks
and the third little pig built himself
a good, strong house.

One day the wolf came knocking
at his door.

"Little pig, little pig," he called.
"Let me come in!"

But the third little pig said:
"No, no, I won't let you in—
not by the hair of my chinny-chin-chin."

"Well then," said the wolf,
"I'll huff and I'll puff
and I'll blow your house down."
So he huffed and he puffed
and he huffed and he puffed . . .
and he huffed and he puffed,
but he just <u>couldn't</u> blow the
house down!

This made the wolf angry, but
he only said, "Little pig, I know
where there's a field of turnips."

"Oh, where?" asked the third little pig.
"Right down the road," said the wolf.
"I'll come for you at ten o'clock
tomorrow morning, and we'll
go together."

The next morning the little pig
got up at nine o'clock and
hurried to the turnip field. He was
back safe in his house when the
wolf came knocking.

"Little pig," said the wolf. "It's
time to go."

"Oh, I already got myself a nice
basket of turnips," the little
pig said.

This made the wolf very angry, but he just said, "Little pig, I know where there's a big apple tree."

"Oh, where?" asked the little pig.

"Across the meadow," said the wolf. "I'll come for you tomorrow at nine o'clock. We'll go together."

The next morning the little pig
got up at eight o'clock. He was
busy picking apples when he
saw the wolf coming.

"Here's an apple for you!"
the little pig called, and he
threw it so far the wolf had to
chase after it. Then the little pig
climbed down and ran away.

As soon as the little pig was safe in his house, the wolf came knocking.

"Little pig," he said, "tomorrow there's going to be a fair in town. I'll come for you at eight o'clock."

The next morning the little pig got up at seven o'clock and hurried to the fair, where he had a good time, until he saw the wolf coming. The little pig jumped into a barrel to hide. But the barrel fell over and rolled down the hill, faster and faster, straight toward the wolf— and it knocked him down!

The little pig was cooking
himself a big pot of soup
when the wolf came banging
on his door. "Little pig," he
called, "I didn't see you at the fair."

"Oh, but I saw you," said the
little pig. "I was riding home in
the barrel that knocked you down."

This made the wolf really angry,
much angrier than before.

"Little pig!" he roared. "I've had enough of your tricks. Now I'm coming to get you." The wolf leaped onto the little pig's roof and he threw himself down the little pig's chimney, and he fell right into the pot of soup and was cooked.

That night, the third little pig
had wolf soup for supper.
 Yumm-yum!

The Three Little Pigs

Meet the Author and Illustrator

Margot Zemach's mother was an actress. She traveled a lot, so Margot lived with her grandparents in Oklahoma. "I have always drawn pictures, all my life," she says. Her daughter, Kaethe, is also an artist.

Theme Connections

Within the Selection

Read the questions below, and think about your answers. In small groups, discuss your ideas with one another. Then choose a person to report your group's answers to the class.

- With what materials was the safest house built?
- How did the third little pig outsmart the wolf?

Across Selections

- What other story tells about a house that keeps out danger?

Beyond the Selection

- Think about the houses in your neighborhood. What are they made of?
- Add items to the Concept/Question Board about homes.

Pronunciation Key

a as in **a**t

ā as in l**a**te

â as in c**a**re

ä as in f**a**ther

e as in s**e**t

ē as in m**e**

i as in **i**t

ī as in k**i**te

o as in **o**x

ō as in r**o**se

ô as in b**o**ught
and r**a**w

oi as in c**oi**n

o͝o as in b**oo**k

o͞o as in t**oo**

or as in f**or**m

ou as in **ou**t

u as in **u**p

ū as in **u**se

ûr as in t**ur**n;
g**er**m, l**ear**n,
f**ir**m, w**or**k

ə as in **a**bout,
chick**e**n, penc**i**l,
cann**o**n, circ**u**s

ch as in **ch**air

hw as in **wh**ich

ng as in ri**ng**

sh as in **sh**op

th as in **th**in

t͟h as in **th**ere

zh as in trea**s**ure

The mark (ʹ) is placed after a syllable with a heavy accent, as in **chicken** (chikʹ ən).
The mark (ˊ) after a syllable shows a lighter accent, as in **disappear** (disˊ ə pērʹ).

262

Glossary

A

above (ə buv′) *prep.* Over; on top of.

absolutely (ab′ sə lo͞ot′ lē) *adv.* Certainly; without any doubt.

admired (ad mīrd′) *adj.* Well thought of.

angry (ang′ grē) *adj.* Mad; upset.

average (av′ ər ij) *adj.* Ordinary; like most others.

B

bang (bang) *n.* A sudden, loud noise.

boa constrictor (bō′ ə kən strik′ tər) *n.* A snake that kills its prey by squeezing.

bog

bog (bog) *n.* A swamp; a marsh.

breathe (brēt͟h) *v.* To take air in and blow air out.

bricklayer (brik′ lā′ ər) *n.* A person who builds walls out of bricks or concrete blocks.

budge (buj) *v.* To move a little bit.

build (bild) *v.* To put together or form.

builder (bil′ dər) *n.* A person who builds or makes things, such as houses.

bulldozer (boॖol′ dō′ zər) *n.* A large machine that a person rides like a tractor while the machine pushes stones, dirt, and trees out of the way.

burrow (bûr′ ō) *n.* A hole or tunnel under the ground that an animal digs to live in.

burst (bûrst) *n.* A small, quick explosion. *v.* To come out suddenly and strongly.

bury (ber′ ē) *v.* To cover from view; to hide by covering.

C

carpenter (kär′ pən tər) *n.* A person who makes things out of wood.

cement (si ment′) *n.* A mixture of sand, water, and crushed stone that dries as hard as stone.

clamp (klamp) *v.* To hold tightly.

claw (klô) *n.* 1. A sharp, curved nail on an animal's foot. 2. The hard, pincher part at the end of a crab's or lobster's legs. *v.* To scratch or pull up by using hands, fingernails, or claws.

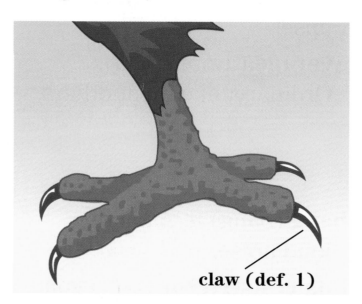

claw (def. 1)

clench (klench) *v.* To close tightly.

clever (klev′ ər) *adj.* Smart.

clumsy (klum′ zē) *adj.* Likely to trip or bump into things.

clunk (klungk) *v.* To hit hard; to make a loud noise.

collection (kə lek′ shən) *n.* A group of things belonging, seen, and kept together.

crash (krash) *n.* 1. A loud noise. 2. A hit or fall.

curds (kûrdz) *n.* Soft balls of cheese; the lumps in cottage cheese.

D

deal (dēl) *n.* A pact; an agreement.

den (den) *n.* A wild animal's home.

den

desert (dez′ ərt) *n.* A large area of very dry land.

driftwood (drift′ wŏŏd) *n.* A piece of wood floating in the water or washed up onto a beach.

droop (drŏŏp) *v.* To bend or curve down.

drown (droun) *v.* To die from being kept under water and not able to breathe air.

duchess (duch′ is) *n.* The wife of a duke.

dwelling (dwel′ ing) *n.* A place to live.

E

electrician (i lek trish′ ən) *n.* A person who puts electrical wires in a building.

enemy (en′ ə mē) *n.* Someone or something that wants to hurt another.

engineer (en′ jə nēr′) *n.* The person who drives a train.

excitement (ik sīt′ mənt) *n.* A mood or feeling of high interest or energy.

exciting (ik sī′ ting) *adj.* Awesome; very interesting.

exclaim (ik sklām′) *v.* To say something suddenly and loudly.

F

farfetching (fär′ fech′ ing) *v.* Exaggerating.

fiddler crab (fid′ lər krab) *n.* A small, round shellfish with one claw larger than the other.

first (fûrst) *adj.* Being ahead of all others; being in the front or beginning.

forest

forest (for′ ist) *n.* A large area of trees.

frightened (frit′ nd) *adj.* Afraid; scared.

G

gather (gat͟h′ ər) *v.* To collect; to bring together.

generally (jen′ ər ə lē) *adv.* Most of the time.

gigantic (jī gan′ tik) *adj.* Very big; huge.

glide (glīd) *v.* To move easily or smoothly.

gloomy (glo͞o′ mē) *adj.* Dark.

goggly (gog′ lē) *adj.* Bulging; staring wide open.

greedy (grē′ dē) *adj.* Not satisfied or happy with what one has; wanting more and better things or money.

H

happily (hap′ ə lē) *adv.* Done with cheer or pleasantness.

hollow (hol′ ō) *n.* A hole; an empty space. *adj.* Empty inside.

howl (houl) *v.* To cry or shout loudly.

huge (hūj) *adj.* Very large.

hungry (hung′ grē) *adj.* Wanting or needing food.

L

lightning (līt′ ning) *n.* A flash of electricity across the sky.

loose (lo͞os) *adj.* Not tightly packed.

M

magnifying glass (mag′ nə fī′ ing glas) *n.* A glass that enlarges the view.

moist (moist) *adj.* A little wet; damp.

N

narrow (nar′ ō) *adj.* Not very wide; close.

nonsense (non′ sens) *n.* Foolishness; silliness.

nursery (nûr′ sə rē) *n.* A room set apart for young animals or babies.

O

office (ô′ fis) *n.* A place where business is done; a place where business people work.

oozy (o͞o′ zē) *adj.* Soft and slimy.

own (ōn) *adj.* Belonging to oneself.

P

pair (pâr) *n.* Two things that are alike or almost alike.

pebble (peb′ əl) *n.* A small stone.

peer (pēr) *v.* To look at something as if studying it.

picture (pik′ chər) *n.* A perfect example.

piece (pēs) *n.* A small part of something.

pleasant (plez′ ənt) *adj.* Nice.

plumber (plum′ ər) *n.* A person who puts water pipes into a building.

pueblo (pweb′ lō) *n.* A group of houses built on top of each other, made of stone or adobe bricks.

poker (pōk′ ûr) *n.* A metal rod for stirring fires.

pueblo

poker

Q

quiver (kwiv′ ər) *v.* To shake; to tremble; to shiver.

R

porch (pôrch) *n.* A covered entrance on the back or front of a house.

problem (prob′ ləm) *n.* A difficult or uncomfortable situation.

protect (prə tekt′) *v.* To keep safe.

reed (rēd) *n.* The stiff stem of a grassy plant that can be woven into mats, baskets, or roofs.

reflection (ri flek′ shən) *n.* The image in a mirror, glass, pond, or puddle.

refuse (ri fūz′) *v.* To say no to something.

s

saucer (sä′ sûr) *n.* A small shallow dish for holding a cup.

saucer

scared (skârd) *adj.* Afraid; frightened; filled with fear.

scramble (skram′ bəl) *v.* To crawl quickly.

scritch-scratch (skrich-skrach) *n.* A soft noise made by dragging or scratching something.

scurry (skur′ ē) *v.* To run quickly.

second (sek′ ənd) *adj.* Being in the number two position; after the first.

shall (shal) *v.* Will.

shelter (shel′ tər) *n.* A place of protection from danger or weather.

shiver (shiv′ ər) *v.* To shake because of fear.

shook (shŏŏk) *v.* Moved back and forth very quickly.

sleek (slēk) *adj.* Smooth.

slinkety-sly (sling′ ki tē slī′) *adj.* In a sneaky way.

snort (snôrt) *v.* To blow air noisily through the nose.

somersault (sum′ ər sôlt′) *n.* A turn that is made by turning head over heels.

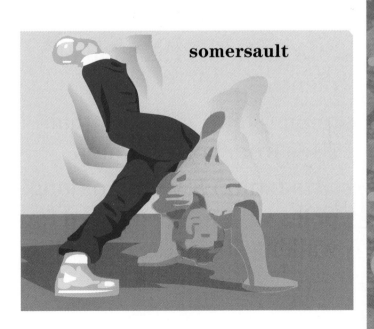

somersault

sometimes (sum′ tīmz) *adv.* At times; part of the time.

spine (spīn) *n.* A stiff, sharp fin on the back of a fish.

spine

squeal (skwēl) *v.* To make a loud, high cry.

stalk (stôk) *n.* The stem of a plant.

steam (stēm) *n.* A mist that rises from boiling water.

stilts (stiltz) *n.* A pair of long poles with footrests used for walking above the ground.

stomach (stum′ ək) *n.* The middle part of a person's body.

straw (strô) *n.* The dried stems of plants.

stumble (stum′ bəl) *v.* To walk in a clumsy way.

suggest (səg jest′) *v.* To tell an idea; to give a plan.

supposed to (sə pōzd′ tōō) *v.* Expected to.

swirl (swûrl) *v.* To spin around quickly.

swirl

T

teddy bear (ted′ ē bâr) *n.* A soft, stuffed toy bear.

third (thûrd) *adj.* In the number three position; after the first and second.

thunder (thun′ dər) *n.* A loud noise heard after lightning.

thunderstorm (thun′ dər storm′) *n.* A storm with thunder and lightning.

tide (tīd) *n.* The rise and fall of the sea.

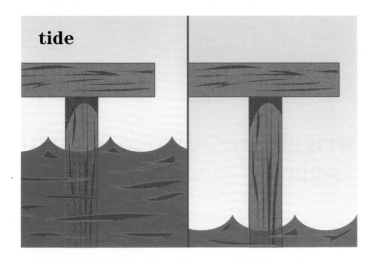

tide

tin (tin) *n.* A kind of metal.

tiptoe (tip′ tō) *v.* To walk on one's toes.

tongue (tung) *n.* Part inside the mouth that helps a person talk.

tough (tuf) *adj.* Strong.

tremble (trem′ bəl) *v.* To shake; to shiver.

troll (trōl) *n.* A small, ugly make-believe creature who often causes trouble.

tuffet (tuf′ it) *n.* A low seat or stool.

turnip (tûr′ nip) *n.* A vegetable with a large, round root that is eaten.

turnip

typical (tip′ i kəl) *adj.* Usual; regular.

U

ugly (ug′ lē) *adj.* Not pleasant looking.

until (un til′) *prep.* Up to a certain time or place.

unusual (un ū′ zhoo əl) *adj.* Strange; rare; different from most others.

usually (ū′ zhoo əl ē) *adv.* Most of the time.

V

vacuum (vak′ ūm) *v.* To clean with a machine that picks up dirt.

W

wavy (wā′ vē) *adj.* Curvy; curly.

where (hwâr) *adj.* In what place; in what location.

whey (hwā) *n.* The watery part of cheese that is left when milk is turned into cheese.

whirl (hwûrl) *v.* To spin around quickly.

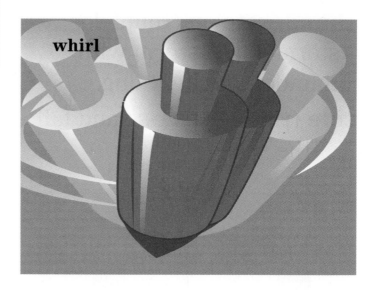

whirl

wriggle (rig′ əl) *v.* To twist; to squirm.

Y

yank (yangk) *v.* To pull quickly and hard.